Pain, Struggles, Love & Happiness

Eutella Nicole

Fulton Books, Inc.
Meadville, PA

Published by Fulton Books 2021

ISBN 978-1-64952-889-6 (paperback)
ISBN 978-1-64952-890-2 (digital)

Printed in the United States of America

Dedication

I dedicate this book of poems to my gifts in life: my husband, Andre Sr.; my children, Sanai, Andre, Olamide, and Nefertede; my brothers, Raphael, Donald, and Damon; my dad, Raphael; and last but not least, my mother; Roberta Maxine.

My mom was very creative and expressed her adult life through her poems in which she wanted to one day have published. Her passing inspired me to also express my feelings through creative writing. I promised myself to grant her wish by allowing the world to hear her voice through her writing.

Introduction

This book of poems are renditions of the pain, struggles, sorrow, love, and happiness my mother, Roberta Maxine, and I, Eutella Nicole, have experienced throughout our lives.

The Pain Within

Why am I so heavy? I can't hardly walk.
I can't stand to look in the mirror or hear my thoughts.
My eyes are weeping, my mind is shot.
My heart is broken and the days are lost.

What can I do? Where can I go?
No one's there to talk to when I'm feeling low.
No one understands, or do they even care?
It's just me, my mind, and the pain I bear.

They say get help, they say go away.
They don't want to be bothered, they say come back another day.
I'm so worried, I'm so scared.
I'm afraid at night 'cause no one's there.

The pain within is truly hard.
I just want to wake up or be dealt another card.

By Roberta Maxine

Looking through the Window

Looking through the window
But there's nothing to see
So I started thinking of the sky
And how it would be.

To go to heaven
To be with God
To finally find
A place where I can be happy
And have a peace of mind.

If there's such a place that is true
Happiness can really shine through
Only with him, that's what they say
So I'll keep searching to find my way
Straight to heaven I hope and I pray
As I continue looking through the window day after day.

By Roberta Maxine

Where Are You

Can you hear me, Father? I'm calling your name
I can't take much more of this heartache and pain
It's hard, it hurts, it's messing me up
I'm so scared and always down
It's turning my life all around.

I can't fight no more with this evil war
They're here, they're there, they are everywhere
The gangs and pain of the violence within them
Makes my heart beat fast.

I try to run, but there is nowhere to hide
No one to talk to, I have too much pride
Where are you, Father, didn't you hear my call?
You promised you would be there for us all.

By Roberta Maxine

Why Me

The wind is howling, what will it do?
I'm afraid, can you hear it too?
Trees are moving all over the place
While water is falling and it's a disgrace.

Papers are flying while cats run and hide
Trying to find a home to stay alive
I've seen it before and it was a total mess
People cleaning for days without any rest.

Many died while others were mad
Mad because they lost all they had
When will it stop and what can we do?
Losing everything in a world such as you
I pray God give me the strength to see it all through.

By Roberta Maxine

Life or Death

Where is my God? When will he come?
I can't take much more of the violence and guns
It happens every day, no matter where you stay
It's really bad, we all need to pray.

Some say it's the government's fault
I wonder where they get their thoughts
How do they expect people to live
When we can't survive with what they provide?

It's a fight for salvation
Only the strong survive
If you don't know God
You're not even alive.

By Roberta Maxine

A Cruel World

It happened one night not long ago
They took my child with a simple blow
They never spoke, they didn't care
They never asked if he was there.

They saw a child and assumed the worse
'Cause he was Black and in the dirt
He must have done it, that's what they said
He fit the profile, and now he's dead.

By Roberta Maxine

Where Am I Going

It's dark outside, I can't hardly see
I can't see my hands nor my feet
The wind is blowing and it's extremely cold
I wonder where I'm going, I'm all alone.

Where is this place? Why did I leave?
The streets are a mess and I can't hardly see
I'm stepping on trash and now I'm dirty.

Where am I going? Can someone help me please?
I know I'm on medication, but it's affecting me.
Oh, wait! Stop! What is this I see?
It's my wonderful angel directing me.

By Roberta Maxine

Tell Jesus

Tell Jesus your troubles, tell him your pain
Let him help you whenever he can
He wants to help in every way
He's calling you and reaching out throughout the day.

He has the power, he's willing to share
He loves us all, he'll always be there
He will bless you and take you far
If you truly love him and give him your heart.

No one else can do it, no one can even come close
He is the master from coast to coast
He has the power to heal and the will to save
But he need the chance to help you change.

By Roberta Maxine

One More Time

One more time, Lord, I'm here one more time.
I'm calling on you to save me one more time.
I can see and hear the doctors discussing my case.
As I look through my window hoping to see your face.
Why can't they understand it's not them who can make me well.
Only you and your gracious favor can bring me through, time will
    tell.

One more time, Lord, I need you one more time.
Set the date and meet me at the appointed place.
Just make sure I see you one more time.
Let me be able to speak your words and see your loving face
As I relax and accept your loving grace.

One more time, Lord, please hear my cry one more time.
I'm praying and asking you to take care of me, one more time.
My trust, belief, and increasing faith is all in your hands.
I'm counting on you, your blessings, and your appointed plan.
To carry me through this unpleasant land.
I know you'll be with me and that you love and care for me too.
So please allow your will to continue to bless me one more time, this
    is my prayer to you.

By Roberta Maxine

When Doors Close

When doors close, where do you go?
Who's there to help or who can you talk to?
We have a Savior, he's our heavenly Father.
His name is Jesus and he loves us so.
He made a promise that will never fail.
We must call on him 'cause he's truly a blessing
He's here for you and for me.
Just open your heart and allow him to come in and do his part.

By Roberta Maxine

A Miracle

A miracle is what this is
How many believe or truly understand
I read his Words and trusted his plan.

I knew it could happen if I just stood still
Listen, trust, and obey, that is his will.

I prayed for the blessings he gave to me
All my pain went away and I was set free.

This is a miracle, I can truly say
I'll continue to thank him every night and every day.

By Roberta Maxine and Eutella Nicole

You Don't Care

You don't care what happens to me
I'm a Black woman with problems, can't you see?
I have no man, no job, or cash
An average woman you walked right past.

I try so hard to better myself
Never held a job, always needed help
Living check to check, nothing left to spend on myself.

Cabinets empty and refrigerator bare
No money left, and my man said he's out of here
I thought he loved me
He told me he'll always be there
But now I know he just didn't care.

By Robert Maxine and Eutella Nicole

You're with Me

Because I woke up to see another day
You're with me
As I travel from point A to point B
You're with me
Being able to deal with any challenges that come my way
You're with me
Treating others with kindness and respect
You're with me
Having a loving family that loves me unconditionally
You're with me
The ability to work and achieve my goals
You're with me
Sustaining a peaceful and comfortable environment
You're with me
Being able to pray and thank you for another day
Thank you, God, for always being there for me!

By Eutella Nicole

I Smile

I smile because you love me
Took me in your arms and allowed me to be free
Free from all fools and negativity
Treated me with respect
Gently directed me when I was incorrect
Never once did I feel neglected
My life is better than I expected
I smile because my life with you is perfect.

By Eutella Nicole

Love Games

Why do people play games in relationships?
Is it the thrill of a chase?
Is it a pretty face that you don't want to replace?
Is it a want for extras in your database or because
you want someone lying on your pillow case?
Do you need someone to help you forget your mistakes?
Or
Do you play games because your heart is filled with empty space?
No trust in a relationship is a disgrace!
Beware of the game players because you might be next in place.

By Eutella Nicole

Thank You

Thank you for being my mommy
Thank you for helping me to make better choices
Thank you for your honesty and integrity
Thank you for allowing me to be the women I turned out to be
Thank you for being a good friend
Thank you for always listening
Thank you for your support and security
Thank you for seeing when I couldn't see
Thank you for the love you have implanted in me
Thank you for choosing Andre for me
Thank you for your constant prayers
Thank you for always being there
I thank God every day for creating you just for me.

By Eutella Nicole

It's a Blessing

It's a blessing to have a nurturing mother who loves you so much,
She put all your needs above hers.
It's a blessing to have a strong, hardworking father
Who takes care his family and his responsibilities.
It's a blessing to experience brotherly love
It's a blessing to have a loving spouse that understands you.
It's a blessing to have the gift of knowledge
There is no comparable blessing like the birth of your child
It's a blessing to have financial stability
It's a blessing to be blessed.

By Eutella Nicole

Always in My Heart

Even though you had to go, you're always in my heart
The feeling of a bitter foe, I hated knowing we had to part

I felt guilty when I smiled, remembering your body so fragile
Miserable, unhappy, and sad, I was so mad

There is a whole in my heart that cannot mend

I cannot believe I lost my best friend

But I know God is with me every day
Helping me to cope with my feelings of dismay
I remembered what you told me: to pray,
trust in God, and be happy

I'll keep you in my heart forever and always.

By Eutella Nicole

Imagine

Imagine the world being a better place to live
Where all people get along and they're not aggressive.
Everyone is greeted with a wonderful smile
We all live a healthy lifestyle.

Imagine we all learned from our parents mistakes
Living happy without any heartaches.
Each mother and father working together as one
Just as I believe it would be in heaven.

Imagine not being boastful with materialistic blings
Putting family first above all things.
Appreciating life for what it supposed to be
Having equality for you and me.

Imagine everyone sewing a seed, reaping what we sow
And living off the proceeds.

Imagine, imagine, imagine!

By Eutella Nicole

My Special Gifts

My mom, whom I miss deeply,
Did everything in her power to make sure we had a stable home.
She kept us safe and happy.

My husband, whom I love passionately,
And appreciate his honesty, compassionate love, and security.

My children, whom I adore,
For their unconditional love and happiness.

My brothers, whom I love, respect and trust.

My dad, whom I admire for his courage and wisdom.

My heavenly Father who gives me
Health and strength and watches over me.

Thank you, God, for all my special gifts.

By Eutella Nicole

I Can't Believe

At times, I felt like I couldn't go on.
I was weak and faint, mad at the world
Couldn't believe I lost one of my favorite girls.

The thought of not being able to hear your voice or ask for advice
Made me realize I didn't have another choice.

I can't believe I am actually going on without you here.
You did everything you could for me.
Teaching me how to love unconditionally.
I felt safe.

It's painful not being able to hug you,
So I seek strength and solace by talking to your photos,
And imagining you're speaking back to me.

Although this has been a mournful journey without you,
God has giving me an unbelievable drive and ability to go on.

I can't believe how much prayer has made a difference in my life.
I thank God I had you in my life.

By Eutella Nicole

Beautiful Is

The birth of a newborn baby
Taking his/her first breath and seeing light for the first time.
Finally being held in the arms of that courageous woman,
Who carried him/her for what seemed like eternity
As they gaze into their mommy's eyes for the first time,
And know they're safe in this new unfamiliar place.
Beautiful Is
The flowers growing in a garden
The whistling of hummingbirds in the morning
The breath of fresh air as the sun rising brightens our earth
The necessity of the rain rejuvenating and
penetrating the earth's grounds.
Beautiful Is
A woman who is a lady
Exhibiting witty, smarts, and wisdom.
A mother's unconditional love for her children
Putting her family needs first at all times.
While understanding the wants and needs of each family member.
A woman's natural strengths and compassion
that she practices every day.
She is a woman, she is a lady, she is a friend,
she is a wife, she is a mom!
Beautiful is Life!
Beautiful is Love!
Beautiful is the Power to Believe!
Beautiful is Health, Strength, and Wisdom!
Beautiful is You!
Beautiful is Me!
Beautiful Is Our Heavenly Father Above "God"

By Eutella Nicole

Don't Rush, Take Your Time

When I was younger
I wished I was at a legal age
Don't rush, take your time.

Who wants house chores
I just wanted them to be done
Don't rush, take your time.

School was once fun
Then it got harder and you can't wait for the last day to come
Don't rush, take your time.

I was so eager to feel love
I decided to jump in a relationship while barely knowing him
How can you know him if you don't even know yourself?
Don't rush, take your time.

"Life is a series of choices
You should always take notes and think with a clear mind
Don't rush, take your time!"

By Eutella Nicole

Inspired

Observing a seed blossom into a beautiful flower
I'm inspired
Watching a carefree child develop into a confident responsible adult
I'm inspired
Discovering the positive changes of our world
today compare to the early 1950s
I'm inspired
Seeing the sunshine with a perfect rainbow
after the rain falls on a gloomy day
I'm inspired
Going through challenges of life and being able to bounce back
I'm inspired
Experiencing an unfortunate crisis and
still being able to stand strong
I'm inspired
Learning the word of God and practicing godly habits
I'm inspired.

By Eutella Nicole

I Wish

Sometimes I wish I was still a little girl without any responsibilities
Being told what to do and how to do it.

Having mommy by my side day in and day out
Made me feel secure
I had no worries

I wish I could see her smile
Hear her voice or give her a hug
But all I have are those precious memories of
My best friend
My role model
My angel
My mom
Oh how I wish.

By Eutella Nicole

The Strength of a Man

What is Strength?

Strength is a man who has the courage to take care of his family.
He gets up every day for work, and even though he had a hard day
He return home and still find time to communicate and play.

Strength is a man who gives his wife and children stability.
He exerts physical stamina and energy on a daily basis.
He is vigorous and powerful but also soft when needed.

Strength is a man who is not afraid to express love.
This man knows the greatest love, he knows God.

By Eutella Nicole

Teach Me

Help me to see
Teach me not to be me
How to open up my mind and think clearly
Teach me how to be
Allow me to be free
Take away the pain and misery
Teach me to be how I'm supposed to be.

By Eutella Nicole

The Power of Rain

The tranquil sound of rain against my windowpane
Helps me to relax my overloaded brain.

Some think of rain as a pain
I think it helps with my migraines.

Please don't complain of the rain
It's a beautiful thing.

It helps to sustain life
That's the power of rain.

By Eutella Nicole

The Walk

"Lose Your Fears and Insecurities and Allow Your
Happiness and Strengths to Guide You."

By Eutella Nicole

Who Am I

I am a strong Black woman
Who appreciates my mother and cherishes
her for the rest of my life.

I am a faithful wife
Who treasures her husband
I'm grateful for his honesty and security
and that he chose me as his wife.

I am a loving mother who adores her children
Who pray they live a stress-free life.

I am a sister
Who respects her brothers and others.

Who am I
I am a woman who thanks God for a wonderful life.

By Eutella Nicole

Stand Tall

They said I wouldn't be nothing
Gossiping with discrimination and bad discussions
But I stand tall.

The fake look upon their faces were not pleasant
Smiling at me and hoping I would crumble and fall
But I stand tall.

I'm not discouraged because that's envy if I recall
I hold my head up high and stand tall
Once again I rise above them all.

By Eutella Nicole

Naive

I didn't believe I was that naive
Thought I was in love, but I was deceived

They didn't give me a blueprint of how it should be
Those red flags, I didn't see

I thought I could teach, but I was a trainee
Inexperienced that was me

They told me it was wrong, but I disagreed
Now my eyes are wide open and I can see

By Eutella Nicole

Three Types of Men

There are three types of men
The one who you trust and call your friend
Tell him your secrets from deep within.

There are three types of men
He's cunning and witty like a marksman
Him I call the sniper
You don't see him nor his gun
But you get the bullet and that's no fun.

There are three types of men
He's honest and straightforward
With an oozing sex appeal
I choose this man because he's my real deal.

By Eutella Nicole

Yearning

I wish you could be more than a father for me
Work hard to support your family
I wish you could stand tall like a tree
With strong roots that's how it should be.

Every child should have consistency
Lots of love and support from his family
A better life for you and for me
That's how God intended it to be.

I wish you were a better father to me
You coming home every night would have been nice to see.

I wish you took care of us like you did your other family
I finally realize life isn't always how it supposed to be.

By Eutella Nicole

Daddy's Little Girl

You gave me lots of hugs and kisses
Showered me with love and made me feel like a princess.

You told me I was beautiful
Even when I thought I wasn't.

Daddy, you always made me feel special
Thank you for loving me and showing me how I should be treated.

With love, respect, and dignity
Thanks for giving your little girl what she needed.

Your daily love and affection taught me
What to look for when I grow up and have my own family.

By Eutella Nicole

A True Friend

A true friend is loving and caring
Tells you the truth even if it hurts
Respects your opinions
Understands you inside out
Accepts you just the way you are
Forgives your rude comments
Recognizes the good in you
Enjoys your company
Never neglects you
Demands your trust, honesty, and true friendship.

By Eutella Nicole

My Father

My father has been with me from the start
He brought me into this world
He's number one in my heart.

My father is with me this I know
He travels with me everywhere I go
He always make me happy when I feel low.

My father is with me through good times and the bad
He understands my every need
He lifts me up when I'm feeling sad.

My father watches over me night and day
He fills my heart with gladness
When it's challenged with dismay.

My father gives me choices and listen when I pray
I love my heavenly Father more and more every day.

By Eutella Nicole

Mother's Gift

We didn't have richest
We didn't have it all
We had our mother's love
The greatest gift of all.

By Eutella Nicole

I Feel You

Although you're not here with me
I hear your voice
I know you leaving wasn't your choice
I feel your presence when I pray
Holding on to your beautiful memories
of solace each and every day.

By Eutella Nicole

Selfishly

You were my everything
You comfort me when I was in pain
I loved you selfishly
We communicated every day
Made every situation seem okay
I loved you selfishly
You was always there when I needed you
Our bond was like crazy glue
I loved you selfishly
We did so many things together
Laughed and cried, I thought you would be here forever
I loved you selfishly
Nothing last forever
At some point we have to learn to let go
But hold on to the beautiful memories
and don't take life for granted
Love unselfishly.

By Eutella Nicole

I Didn't See You

I didn't see you throughout my trials and tribulations
I didn't see you when my heart was broken
I didn't see you when I cried at night
I didn't see because I wanted to fight
I didn't see you throughout my accomplishments
I couldn't even hear your voice
Now that my ears are clear and my eyes are open,
I realize you were here the whole time.

By Eutella Nicole

Set Me Free

Set me free from adversaries
Set me free from insecurities
Set me free from dishonesty
Set me free from selfishness
Set me free from my anger
Set me free from my guilt
Set me free from my fears
Set me free from all negativities
Set me free from the pain and misery.

By Eutella Nicole

Teach Me

Teach me how to think
With a clear mind.

Teach me what to say
With a positive loud voice.

Teach me how to act
When a negative situation occurs.

Teach me to treat others
The way I expect to be treated.

Teach me how to be
The best mother and wife.

Teach me what is needed
To have a great life.

By Eutella Nicole

A Mother-Daughter Bond

There is no bond like a mother-daughter bond
I felt this connection from I was a little girl
And it only manifested throughout the years
You taught me to be a lady
To keep my head up
And be strong even when unseeing challenges occurred
I experienced your gift of multitasking
You played many different roles in my life
Yes, you were my mother
But you often had to play the role of my father
A sister and a friend
You were always there for me
You were my second pair of eyes
It was like having a twin sister who knew what I was feeling
I felt your pain and struggles
And tried to be the person you needed me to be
I know being a single parent with three children was a struggle
But you did a great job!
When my heart feels heavy, I sit back relax
and think of our special bond
It give me a sense of peace
I pray my daughter and I can one day
experience a mother-daughter bond
I thank God and I thank you for this special gift.

By Eutella Nicole

Missing You

I still can't believe that you are gone
The shock of losing you left me torn
I know they say one have to mourn
I often wish I was just born.

What can I do to make this pain go away
I laugh, cry, and pray
Something, anything for a better day.

I need to feel your presence
Don't know what to do
I just have your memory of solace
I will never stop missing you.

By Eutella Nicole

Wasn't Prepared

I thought I was doing all I could
Getting the right information is what I understood.

That call at 11:02 p.m., January 10, 2012, was a fright
I screamed out, "No! It's not fair. It's not right."

What happened? You were fine
Now all of a sudden, your life is on the line.

They stumbled all over their words
I often wonder if they paid attention to what really occurred.

You said to trust and believe when you pray
That, I will always obey.

The memory of it all will always be unclear
Losing you, *no, I wasn't prepared.*

By Eutella Nicole

About the Author

Roberta Maxine was a single parent with three children. She received her bachelor's degree in education at the College of New Rochelle in the Bronx. She was a first-grade school teacher who loved working with children and practiced her imaginative talents in arts, crafts, and poetry.

Eutella Nicole have always loved to write and express her creative thoughts on papers written in early school days and throughout college. Eutella was inspired to write poems on January 10, 2012. The day God called her mother, Roberta Maxine, home. Eutella Nicole's way of coping with her mother's death was through her creative writing. She no longer had her mom to talk to, so she expressed herself by writing poems. Over the years, Eutella realized writing was not only an outlet, but she had developed a spiritual passion and zeal for poetry.

CPSIA information can be obtained
at www.ICGtesting.com
Printed in the USA
BVHW081435290421
606129BV00009B/845